THE GOSPEL

OF

Jesus' Prophetic Wisdom

THE GOSPEL OF

Jesus' Prophetic Wisdom

by Mark M. Mattison

Also by Mark M. Mattison

The Gospel of Mary:
A Fresh Translation and Holistic Approach

The Gospel of Judas:
The Sarcastic Gospel

The Gospel of Thomas:
A New Translation for Spiritual Seekers

First Edition

Scripture quotations marked DFV are from the *Divine Feminine Version* (DFV) of the New Testament, made publicly available through the Creative Commons License – Attribution, Noncommercial, Share Alike 3.0 United States. For full details see:
http://creativecommons.org/licenses/by-nc-sa/3.0/us

Contents

Acknowledgements

I'd like to express my gratitude to all the women and men of the Grand Rapids Writer's Exchange who have played such an important role in my journey as a writer over the last nine years. Their constructive criticism of my writing has been invaluable.

Particular thanks are due to those writers and readers who commented on the entire manuscript: Karen Jacobs, Daniel June, Jeremy Martin, Wes Thompson, Gregory Hartzler-Miller, Deborah Saxon, Shawna R.B. Atteberry, and David A. Hewitt.

Most of all, I'm deeply grateful to my wife, Rebecca, whose graceful and patient encouragement is a source of inexhaustible spiritual strength.

Introduction

The Gospels of Matthew, Mark, Luke, and John – the opening books of the canonical New Testament – have long been Christians' primary source of knowledge about Jesus and his teachings. But these were not the only Gospels written in the decades and centuries following Jesus. Within the last hundred years, archaeologists and biblical scholars have discovered and studied many others. Some of those texts had been known only by name; others had been entirely lost to history until just recently.[1]

In 1896, a German scholar purchased an ancient Egyptian manuscript from an antiquities dealer in Cairo. As it turned out, the manuscript included the Gospel of Mary, a fifth-century translation of an earlier Greek text. In the years that followed, two third-century Greek fragments of Mary also came to light.

The next year, in 1897, Greek fragments of another unknown Gospel were first published. It wasn't until 1945 that a complete copy was discovered in Egypt. That text turned out to be the long-lost Gospel of Thomas. It was discovered alongside other previously unknown books, including the Gospel of Philip.

Even more recently, sometime in the 1970s (the exact date is unknown), another Gospel was discovered in Egypt, although it wasn't restored and published until 2006 (additional fragments were recovered in 2010). This ancient text turned out to be another one known to have once existed: the controversial Gospel of Judas.

The rapidly increasing number of ancient Gospels available for study has expanded our appreciation of the spiritual breadth and diversity of the many early communities committed to following Jesus. At the same time, in their meticulous study of the canonical Gospels, scholars have also reconstructed the earliest of them all: The Gospel of Q.

"Q" comes from the German word *Quelle*, meaning "source." Specifically, the term "Q" describes a shared literary source used by Matthew and Luke. Its existence was first theorized by a German scholar named Christian Weisse in 1838.[2] The theory is based on the now widely-accepted fact that Mark was written before Matthew, Luke, and John, which (as we'll see) explains much about the literary relationship between the New Testament's Gospels. However, it doesn't explain all the literary parallels.

For its part, John doesn't overlap the others very much.[3] Its content resembles that of Matthew, Mark, and Luke only about eight percent of the time. Put differently, about 92% of John is unique to John. However, the first three canonical Gospels – Matthew, Mark, and Luke – are often referred to collectively as "the Synoptics" since their contents frequently overlap, often word-for-word. Many of these word-for-word agreements are easily explained by the fact that the authors of Matthew and Luke copied and edited large portions of Mark. However, that leaves well over 200 parallel verses that appear in both Matthew and Luke, but not in Mark – almost all of them sayings of Jesus.

If we can explain most of the parallels between Matthew, Mark, and Luke by the dependence of Matthew and Luke on Mark, how are we to explain the parallels between Matthew and Luke that don't appear in Mark? The suggestion that initially emerged in the nineteenth century was that in addition to Mark's Gospel, Matthew and Luke used another common source, now lost to us, which was comprised mainly of a list of Jesus' sayings – the hypothetical "Q" document.

Prior to the discovery of Thomas, the idea of such a document was only theoretical. However, the more recently discovered Gospel of Thomas appears to be exactly the sort of Gospel that scholars believe Q was – a collection of Jesus' sayings, remnants of an oral tradition preserved by Jesus' earliest followers, and passed down from one generation to the next. The discovery of Thomas' Gospel, then, gave greater credence to the theory that other lists of Jesus' sayings – lists like the one now known as Q – circulated among early followers of Jesus.

As Chapter One will describe in greater detail, the lost Gospel of Q, reconstructed from its inclusion in Matthew and Luke, is in fact the first written Gospel known to have existed. It's difficult to overstate the significance of this fact. Since the reconstructed Q is a Gospel in its own right – and the earliest known one at that – it promises not only to complement our understanding of the other Gospels, it promises also to add to our understanding of Jesus himself. When and where was Q written, and what more can we learn from it?

1
The Context of Q

The date, provenance, and development of the Q Gospel has understandably been the subject of some debate, although scholars broadly agree about its general outline.

Whereas Q (or at least some of Q) could have come to Matthew and Luke in the form of oral tradition, these non-Markan texts are so similar to one another in Greek that they're unlikely to have been passed down in oral form. It's even less likely that Jesus' sayings would have been translated from Aramaic into Greek using exactly the same words and passed along by word of mouth to Matthew and Luke. Consequently, Q must have been a written document, probably written in Greek, like the canonical Gospels.

Scholars also widely agree that this Greek collection of Jesus' sayings was written sometime between 50 and 70 C.E., most likely in Galilee. They recognize that Q, like other Gospels, probably went through multiple levels of editing before reaching a final form. John S. Kloppenborg proposed a now widely-held theory about three different editorial stages in Q's development.[1]

Not everyone, however, remains as confident about the possibility of accurately identifying specific editorial layers in a reconstructed hypothetical document.[2] For example, in his foundational book *The New Testament and the People of God*, British scholar N.T. Wright describes the thesis in some detail and raises plausible questions about the entire enterprise.[3] Wright argues that conclusions drawn from the theoretical stratification of this hypothetical document coincide too neatly with a specific agenda to re-envision early Christians who did not believe in things like the resurrection of Jesus – Christians who originally believed in wisdom without prophecy, general ethical teachings without judgment;[4] in short, a type of Jesus-movement which challenges Christianity as it has been traditionally understood and practiced.

This debate over whether Q undermines traditional Christianity is the same debate that "liberal" and "evangelical" scholars have waged for years over Thomas' Gospel.[5] And the position about Q taken here is much like the "moderating" position described in *The Gospel of Thomas: A New Translation for Spiritual Seekers;* that is, Q can be read in such a way as to complement and broaden our understanding of early Christianity without necessarily undermining Christian faith.[6]

True, Wright's criticism does suggest that elaborate attempts to reconstruct the evolution of a document which itself is a reconstruction may fail to pass the test of Ockham's razor. He concludes by expressing sympathy for a simpler explanation of the non-Markan parallels between Matthew and Luke: the theory that "Luke simply used Matthew."[7] If Luke was familiar with both Mark and Matthew, then the non-Markan overlaps between Matthew and Luke wouldn't require a hypothetical source document; those 200-plus verses would simply reflect places where Luke departed from Mark's text and chose to use material from Matthew instead.

The problem with this explanation is that in order to be persuasive, it has to account for why Luke appears to have been unaware of Matthew's editorial revisions to Mark.[8] Though specialists continue to argue the point, the majority of scholars agree that the Q hypothesis is the best way to make sense of all the evidence.

The "middle" position taken here is consistent with the scholarly consensus, but cautious about increasingly elaborate theories. Though reluctant to separate Q into discrete layers of developing tradition, this translation closely follows the most authoritative textual reconstruction, that of the International Q Project, which published *The Critical Edition of Q* in 2000.[9] In addition, the conclusions drawn about the beliefs of those who read and used Q will tend to be more modest in scope. This caution seems warranted since the reconstructed text of Q remains fragmentary. Unless an actual copy of Q is discovered, whatever contents weren't used by both Matthew and Luke will remain unknown.

Though Q appears to have been mainly a list of Jesus' sayings with little or no narrative context (the main exceptions being the temptation story and the story of the Roman centurion), it may have contained other stories as well.[10] Even if it didn't, however, we may still be cautious about assuming that the people who used it didn't believe Jesus rose from the dead. In fact, we know for certain that at least two readers (and editors) of Q did believe in the resurrection of Jesus: The authors of Matthew and Luke.[11] So although Q can (and should) be read as a Gospel about Jesus on its own terms and in its own right, we would be equally justified in refraining from overly elaborate conclusions. Again, the unique perspective of Q could very well be a welcome opportunity to expand and nuance our understanding of the early Jesus movement. Chapters Three through Five will make exactly that point.

Before proposing some of those conclusions, however, it will be helpful to review Q as reconstructed by the most authoritative critical edition. Two translations are included here. The more literal translation in the Appendix retains chapter and verse numbers from Luke and Matthew. Since scholars believe Luke preserves the original chronology of Q more closely than Matthew, most of the verses retain the numbers used in Luke. References to specific verses in Q, then, are often enumerated like "Q 6:36," meaning the verse has been reconstructed by comparing Luke 6:36 with its textual parallel in Matthew 5:48. The more literal translation in the Appendix is being committed to the public domain, and may be freely copied and used for any purpose.

By contrast, the translation in Chapter Two is a slightly more colloquial, "loose" translation intended to make the text accessible. It avoids technical jargon and reads more smoothly. In order to give the sense of the original text, it dispenses with chapter and verse numbers, and also includes headers to help organize the text into logical sections. The very act of organizing the text in such a way is itself an act of interpretation, which is why the more exact translation in the Appendix doesn't contain headers.

Both translations use various strategies to mitigate masculine generic language, but the "loose" version occasionally takes an extra step in that direction (such as adding the word "sister" alongside "brother" in Q 6:41, 42 and Q 17:3). Additionally, the translation in Chapter Two doesn't use the word "Father" to describe God, using the more gender-neutral (yet descriptive) term "Provider" instead.[12] The intent is to convey the sense of the original text as much as possible while avoiding gender-exclusive language.

2
The Gospel of Q:
A New Translation

John the Baptizer

John [...] the entire region around the Jordan [...]
He told the crowds who went out to be baptized, "You offspring of vipers, who warned you to flee from the fury to come? So bear fruit worthy of change! Don't start to say to yourselves, 'We have Abraham for our ancestor,' because I tell you that God is able to raise up children for Abraham from these stones.

"Even now the axe lies at the root of the trees! So every tree that doesn't bear good fruit is cut down and thrown into the fire.

"I baptize you in water, but one who's greater than I will come, the thong of whose sandals I'm not worthy to loosen. He'll baptize you in holy Spirit and fire. His pitchfork is in his hand to clean out his threshing floor, and to gather the wheat into his barn; but he'll burn up the chaff with a fire that can't be put out."

God's Son Initiated

[...] Jesus [...] baptized [...] heaven opened and [...] the Spirit [...] on him [...] Son [...]
Jesus was led by the Spirit into the desert to be tested by the devil. He didn't eat anything for forty days [...] he was hungry.

"If you're God's Son," the devil told him, "tell these stones to turn into bread."

"It's written, 'Don't live on bread alone,'" Jesus replied.

The devil led him to Jerusalem, set him on the pinnacle of the temple, and said, "If you're God's Son, throw yourself down, because it's written, 'God will put angels in charge of you,' and 'On their hands they'll bear you up, so that you don't dash your foot against a stone.'"

"It's been said, 'Don't test the Lord, your God,'" Jesus replied.

Then the devil took him to a very high mountain and showed him all the glorious empires of the world. "I'll give you all these," the devil told him, "if you'll bow to me."

"It's written: 'Bow to the Lord your God, and serve God only,'" Jesus replied.

Then the devil left him.

Jesus' Wisdom Path

[...] Nazareth [...]

He looked up at his disciples and said:

> Blessed are you who are poor,
> because yours is God's reign.

> Blessed are you who are hungry,
> because you'll be full.

> Blessed are you who mourn,
> because you'll be comforted.

"Blessed are you when they criticize you, harass you, and spread lies about you because of the Human One. Rejoice and be glad, because your heavenly reward is great; for that's how they harassed the prophets before you.

"Love your enemies, and pray for those who harass you. You'll become children of your Provider, who makes the sun rise on those who do evil and those who do good, and sends rain on those who are just and those who are unjust.

"When someone slaps you on the cheek, offer the other one too. When someone sues you for your shirt, give them your coat too. When someone makes you go one mile, go an extra mile. Give to everyone who asks you, and when someone borrows your things, don't ask for them back.

"Treat people how you want them to treat you. If you love those who love you, why should you be rewarded? Don't even toll collectors do that? And if you lend to those from whom you expect repayment, why should you be rewarded? Don't people from other nations do that? Be merciful, just like your Provider.

"Don't judge, and you won't be judged; because you'll be judged the way that you judge. And you'll be measured the way that you measure.

"Can someone who can't see guide another person who can't see? Won't they both fall into a pit? A disciple isn't greater than their teacher. It's enough for the disciple to become like their teacher.

"Why do you see the speck that's in your brother's or sister's eye, but don't consider the beam that's in your own eye? How can you tell your brother or sister, 'Let me get that speck out of your eye,' when you don't see the beam that's in your own eye? You hypocrite! First get the beam out of your own eye, and then you'll see clearly to get the speck out of your brother's or sister's eye.

"No good tree bears rotten fruit, nor does a rotten tree bear good fruit. Every tree is known by its own fruit. Are figs gathered from thorns, or grapes from thistles? The person who does good brings good things out of their good treasure, and the person who does evil brings evil things out of evil treasure, because one's mouth speaks from the overflow of the heart.

"Why do you call me, 'Master, Master,' and don't do what I say? Everyone who hears my words and acts on them can be compared to someone building a house on bedrock. When the rain poured, and the floods came, and the winds blew and pounded that house, it didn't collapse, because it was founded on bedrock. But everyone who hears my words and doesn't act on them is like someone who built a house on the sand. When the rain poured, and the floods came, and the winds blew and pounded that house, it collapsed immediately. How great was its fall!"

A Centurion's Trust

And so when he had finished saying these things, he went to Capernaum. A centurion approached and begged him. "My boy is sick," he said.

"I'll go heal him," Jesus said.

"Master," the centurion replied, "I'm not worthy for you to come under my roof. Just say the word, and my boy will be healed. I'm also in a chain of command, with soldiers under me. I tell one, 'Go,' and they go; I tell another, 'Come,' and they come; I tell my servant, 'Do this,' and they do it."

Jesus was amazed when he heard this. He told his followers, "I'm telling you the truth: I haven't found such trust even in Israel."

John and Jesus

When John heard all these things, he sent his disciples to ask him, "Are you the coming one, or should we look for someone else?"

"Go and tell John what you've heard and seen," he replied. "Those who:

> are blind, regain their sight;
> have challenges of mobility, walk;
> have leprosy, are cured;
> are deaf, hear;
> are dead, are raised up;
> are poor, have good news announced to them.

Blessed is the one who isn't scandalized by me."

When they had left, he started to talk to the crowds about John. "What did you go out into the desert to see? A reed shaken by the wind? Then what did you go out to see? A man wearing fancy clothes? Look, those who wear fancy clothes live in palaces. Then what did you go out to see? A prophet? Yes, I'm telling you, and much more than a prophet, because it's written about him:

> Look, I'm sending my messenger ahead of you,
> who'll prepare your path for you.

"I'm telling you that John is greater than anyone who's been born, but whoever is least in God's reign is still greater than he, because John came to you [...] the toll collectors and [...] but [...] him.

"To what, then, can I compare this generation? What's it like? It's like children sitting in the marketplaces calling to each other:

> We played the flute for you,
> but you didn't dance.
> We mourned,
> But you didn't weep.

"John didn't come eating or drinking, and you say, 'He's demonized!' The Human One has come eating and drinking, and you say, 'Look, a glutton and a drunk, a friend of toll collectors and outsiders!' But Wisdom is vindicated by her children."

Following Jesus

Someone told him, "I'll follow you wherever you go."

"Foxes have holes and birds of the sky have nests," Jesus replied, "but the Human One has nowhere to rest his head."

But someone else told him, "Master, let me go and bury my father first."

"Follow me," he replied, "and let the dead bury their own dead."

He told his disciples, "The harvest is plentiful, but the workers are few. So ask the Lord of the harvest to send workers into the fields. Go! Look, I send you out like lambs among wolves. Don't carry a purse, bag, sandals, or staff. Don't greet anyone on the road. Whenever you enter a house, first say, 'Peace to this house.' If a peaceful person is there, let your blessing rest on them; but if not, take back your blessing. Stay in the same house, eating and drinking whatever they give you, because the worker is worthy of their wages. Don't move around from house to house. If they welcome you in whatever town you enter, eat whatever is set before you. Heal those who are sick there and tell them, 'God's reign is at hand!' But if they don't welcome you in whatever town you enter, when you're leaving that town, shake the dust from your feet. I'm telling you that on that day, it'll be better for Sodom than for that town!

"How awful for you, Chorazin! How awful for you, Bethsaida! If the great deeds done in your midst had been done in Tyre and Sidon, they would have changed a long time ago in sackcloth and ashes. But it will be better for Tyre and Sidon than for you in the judgment! And you, Capernaum, you don't think you'll be exalted to heaven, do you? You'll fall down to the grave!

"Whoever welcomes you welcomes me, and whoever welcomes me welcomes the one who sent me."

God as Provider

Then he said, "Thank you, Provider, Lord of heaven and earth, for hiding these things from the wise and learned and revealing them to children. Yes, Provider, this was what you wanted. My Provider has given me everything. No one knows who the child is except the Provider, or who the Provider is except the child, and the one to whom the child wants to reveal.

"Blessed are the eyes that see what you see. I'm telling you that many prophets and rulers wanted to see what you see, but didn't see it; and to hear what you hear, but didn't hear it.

"When you pray, say:

Provider,
We honor your holy name.
Let your reign come.
Give us our daily bread today.
Forgive us our debts,
because we too forgive everyone who's indebted to us.
Don't put us in harm's way.

"I'm telling you, ask and you'll receive. Look and you'll find. Knock and it'll be opened for you, because everyone who asks receives. The one who looks finds. To one who knocks it'll be opened. Which of you would give your child a stone if they ask for bread? Or who would give them a snake if they ask for fish? So if you, evil as you are, know how to give good gifts to your children, how much more will the heavenly Provider give good things to those who ask!"

Overcoming Demonic Power

He was casting out a demon that couldn't speak. Now when the demon came out, the person who couldn't speak started talking. The crowds were amazed. But some said, "He casts out demons with the power of Beelzebul, the ruler of the demons!"

Knowing what they were thinking, he told them, "Every divided empire is devastated, and a divided house will fall. If the Enemy is divided, how will its empire endure? But if Beelzebul gives me power to cast out demons, who gives your people power to cast them out? So they prove you wrong. But if I cast out demons by the finger of God, then God's reign has come to you!

"Whoever isn't with me is against me, and whoever doesn't gather with me, scatters. When the impure spirit leaves someone, it journeys through arid places looking for rest, but doesn't find it. Then it says, 'I'll return to the home I left'; and when it comes back, it finds it swept and organized. Then it goes out and brings seven other spirits that are even more evil, and they move in and live there. That person ends up even worse off than before."

The Coming Judgment

Some demanded him to show a sign. But he said, "This is an evil generation. It demands a sign, but no sign will be provided except the sign of Jonah! As Jonah became a sign to the Ninevites, so the Human One will be a sign to this generation. The queen of the South will rise up in the judgment with this generation and will condemn it, because she came from the ends of the earth to hear Solomon's wisdom; and look, something greater than Solomon is here. The people of Nineveh will rise up in the judgment with this generation and will condemn it, because they changed in response to Jonah's announcement, and look, something greater than Jonah is here.

"No one lights a lamp and hides it, but puts it on a lampstand, and it enlightens everyone in the house. Your eye is the body's lamp. If your eye is focused, your whole body is full of light. If you have an evil eye, your whole body is dark. So if the light within you is dark, how dark it is!

"How awful for you Pharisees! You set aside ten percent of your herbs and spices, but you ignore justice, mercy, and trust. You should've done these without ignoring the others.

"How awful for you Pharisees! You clean the outside of the cup and dish, but inside they're full of greed and decadence. Clean the inside of the cup, and its outside will be clean too.

"How awful for you Pharisees! You love the place of honor at banquets, the front seat in the synagogues, and accolades in the marketplaces. How awful for you, because you're like unmarked graves that people walk on without knowing it.

"And how awful for you lawyers! You load people with burdens that are hard to bear, but you yourselves won't even lift a finger to help them.

"How awful for you lawyers! You shut people out of God's reign. You didn't enter, and didn't let those enter who are trying to do so.

"How awful for you, because you build the tombs of the prophets whom your ancestors killed. The fruit doesn't fall far from the tree. So Wisdom said, 'I'll send prophets and sages. Some of them they'll kill and harass.' So this generation will be guilty of the blood of all the prophets shed from the beginning of the world, from the blood of Abel to the blood of Zechariah, who died between the altar and the sanctuary. Yes, I'm telling you that this generation will be held responsible.

"Nothing is concealed that won't be revealed, nor hidden that won't be made known. Whatever I tell you in the dark, say in the light; and whatever you hear whispered in your ear, announce from the housetops.

"Don't be afraid of those who kill the body but can't kill the soul. Instead, fear the one who can kill both the soul and the body in the burning trash heap.

Priorities

"Don't five sparrows cost two pennies? Yet not one of them will fall to the ground without your Provider's permission. Even the hairs of your head are all numbered. Don't be afraid, because you're more valuable than many sparrows.

"Everyone who publicly acknowledges me, the Human One will acknowledge in front of the angels. But whoever publicly denies me will be denied in front of the angels. Whoever speaks out against the Human One will be forgiven, but whoever speaks out against the holy Spirit won't be forgiven. When they bring you before the synagogues, don't worry about how or what you should say, because the holy Spirit will teach you at that time what you should say.

"Don't store treasures for yourselves here on earth, where moth and rust destroy and robbers break in and steal. Instead, store treasures for yourselves in heaven, where neither moth nor rust destroy and where robbers don't break in or steal. Because where your treasure is, there your heart will be too.

"So I'm telling you not to worry about your life, about what you'll eat; or about your body, what you'll wear. Isn't life more than food, and the body more than clothes? Think about how the ravens don't sow, reap, or gather into barns, yet God feeds them. Aren't you more valuable than the birds?

"Which of you can grow any taller by worrying? And why worry about clothes? Look at how the lilies grow. They don't work or spin, yet I'm telling you that even Solomon in all his glory wasn't dressed like one of these. But if God clothes the grass of the field, which is here today and is thrown into the oven tomorrow, won't God clothe you even more, you who have little trust? So don't worry. Don't ask, 'What are we going to eat?' or 'What are going to drink?' or 'What are we going to wear?' People from other nations look for all these things, but your Provider knows that you need all of them. Instead, look for God's reign, and all these things will be given to you too.

"But know this: If the master of the house had known at what time the robber was coming, he wouldn't have let his house be broken into. You too should be ready, because the Human One is coming when you don't expect it.

"Then who is the trustworthy and wise servant who was entrusted by their master to hand out rations to the household at the right time? Blessed is that servant whose master finds them doing so when he comes. I'm telling you the truth: he'll put them in charge of all that he owns. But if that servant says in their heart, 'My master is late,' and starts to beat the other servants and to eat and drink with those who are addicted to alcohol, the master of that servant will come when they don't expect it, at a time that they don't know, and will rip them to shreds and throw them out with those who are untrustworthy.

"I came to cast fire on the earth, and how I wish it were already kindled! Do you think that I came to bring peace on earth? I didn't come to bring peace, but a sword! Because I've come:

> To pit son against father,
> daughter against her mother,
> daughter-in-law against her mother-in-law."

He told them, "When it's evening, you say, 'There'll be good weather, because the sky is red.' In the morning, 'There'll be wintry weather today, because the sky is red and threatening.' You know how to interpret the appearance of the sky. Why don't you know how to interpret the time?

"When you're going with your adversary, do your best to settle the case on the way there, or else your adversary may hand you over to the judge, and the judge to the officer, and the officer may throw you into prison. I'm telling you that you won't get out of there until you've paid the very last penny!

Entering God's Reign

"What is God's reign like, and to what should I compare it? It can be compared to a mustard seed which someone sowed in their garden. It grew and became a tree, and the birds of the sky nested in its branches."

"And again: To what should I compare God's reign? It can be compared to yeast which a woman hid in fifty pounds of flour until it was all fermented.

"Enter through the narrow door, because many will try to enter, though only a few will succeed. When the master of the house gets up and locks the door, you'll be standing outside and knocking on it. 'Master, open up for us!' you'll say.

"But he'll reply, 'I don't know you.'

"Then you'll start to say, 'We ate and drank with you, and you taught in our streets.'

"But he'll say, 'I don't know you. Go away, you criminals!'

"Many will come from east and west and dine with Abraham, Isaac, and Jacob in God's reign, but you'll be thrown out into the outer darkness, where there'll be weeping and grinding of teeth. Those who are last will be first, and those who are first will be last.

"Jerusalem, Jerusalem, who kills the prophets and stones those who are sent to her! How often I would've gathered your children together, like a hen gathers her chicks under her wings, but you wouldn't let me! Look, your house is left abandoned. I'm telling you that you won't see me until the time comes when you say, 'Blessed is the one who comes in the name of the Lord!'

"Whoever exalts themselves will be humbled, and whoever humbles themselves will be exalted.

"Someone planning a great dinner invited many guests. When dinner was ready, they sent their servant to tell the invited guests, 'Come, because it's ready now!'

"One excused himself because of his farm. Another excused himself because of his business. The servant went back and told their master all this. Then the master of the house got mad and told the servant, 'Go out to the highways and urge people to come in so that my house may be filled.'

"Whoever doesn't disregard father and mother can't be my disciple, and whoever doesn't disregard son and daughter can't be my disciple. Whoever doesn't carry their own cross and follow me can't be my disciple.

"Whoever tries to find their life will lose it, but whoever loses their life for my sake will find it.

"Salt is good, but if it's lost its flavor, how can you get it back? It's no good for the soil or the manure pile. It's thrown away.

"No one can follow two masters, because they'll either hate one and love the other, or they'll be devoted to one and despise the other. You can't serve both God and money.

"The Torah and the prophets were announced until John. Since then, God's reign has been violated, and the violent plunder it. But it's easier for heaven and earth to disappear than for one smallest letter or one tiny pen stroke to drop out of the Torah.

"Everyone who divorces his wife and remarries is unfaithful to her, and whoever marries someone who's divorced is unfaithful too.

"There's no way that people won't be tripped up, but how awful it will be for anyone who causes it! It'd be better for them if a millstone were hung around their neck and they were thrown into the sea, than for them to trip up one of these little ones.

"Which of you, if you had a hundred sheep and lost one of them, wouldn't leave the ninety-nine in the hills and go after the one that got lost? When they find it, I'm telling you that they'll rejoice over it more than over the ninety-nine that didn't wander off.

"Or what woman with ten silver coins, if she loses one, wouldn't light a lamp, sweep the house, and look everywhere until she found it? When she finds it, she calls together her friends and neighbors. 'Rejoice with me,' she says, 'because I've found the coin that I'd lost!' In the same way, I'm telling you, the angels rejoice over one wrongdoer who changes.

"If your brother or sister offends you, correct them. If they change, forgive them. Even if they offend you seven times a day, then forgive them seven times.

"If you had trust as big as a mustard seed, you could tell this mulberry tree, 'Be uprooted and be planted in the sea,' and it would obey you."

The Coming of God's Reign

He was asked when God's reign would come. "The coming of God's reign can't be observed," he replied. "Nor will they say, 'Look over here!' or 'Look over there!' Because look, God's reign is among you.

"If they tell you, 'Look, he's in the desert!' don't go out; or 'Look, he's inside,' don't follow, because as the lightning flashes in the east and is seen in the west, so will the Human One be in his day. Where there's a corpse, there the vultures will gather.

"As it was in the days of Noah, so it will be in the day of the Human One. In those days they were eating and drinking, marrying and giving in marriage, until the day that Noah entered the ark, and the flood came and swept all of them away. That's what it will be like on the day the Human One is revealed.

"I'm telling you, there'll be two men in the field; one will be taken and the other will be left. There'll be two women grinding at the mill; one will be taken and the other will be left.

"A certain person went on a trip. He called ten of his servants and gave them ten minas. 'Do business with this until I return,' he told them.

"After a long time the master of those servants returned to settle accounts with them. The first one came and said, 'Master, your mina has made ten more minas.'

"He said, 'Well done, good servant! Since you've been trustworthy with a little, I'll put you in charge of much.'

"The second came and said, 'Master, Your mina has made five minas.'

"He said, 'Well done, good servant! Since you've been trustworthy with a little, I'll put you in charge of much.'

"The other came and said, 'Master, I know you're a strict man, reaping where you didn't sow and gathering where you didn't scatter. I went out and hid your mina in the ground. Look, here's what belongs to you!'

"He said, 'You evil servant! You knew that I reap what I didn't sow and gather where I didn't scatter? So why didn't you invest my money with the bankers? Then when I returned, I would've gotten it back, with interest. So take the mina away from him and give it to the one who has ten minas, because everyone who has will be given more, but whoever doesn't have will lose even what little they do have.'

"You who've followed me will sit on thrones, judging the twelve tribes of Israel."

3
The Historical Jesus and Q

Since Q is our earliest known Gospel, it's reasonable to ask what it may be able to tell us about the historical Jesus himself. To what degree may Q afford us a glimpse into the actual words and deeds of Jesus from Nazareth in the 30s C.E.?

This isn't an easy question to answer. The consensus of mainstream biblical scholars is that no one who wrote any of the Gospels actually knew Jesus: Not the author(s) or editor(s) of Q, nor the authors of Mark, Matthew, Luke, John, Thomas, Mary, etc.; for that matter, not even Paul, although Paul did meet some of Jesus' disciples on at least three occasions.[1] What we do have are Gospels written decades after Jesus' life and death, texts which document oral traditions handed down for generations from Jesus and his earliest followers.

The Gospels about Jesus, then, do preserve actual sayings of the historical Jesus (oral traditions), although they've been shaped and edited according to the theological concerns of specific communities of faith in particular times and places.

Put differently, traditional sayings of Jesus are preserved in first- and second-century Gospels in narrative stories that blend history with theology. This is not at all to discount the significance or meaning of these various Gospels in their own contexts, or to suggest that the spiritual insights they offer are any less meaningful for us today. However, it does mean that none of the Gospels presents literal "history" in the modern sense of biographies with precise details about dates, times, places, transcripts, recordings, etc. To expect otherwise would be to hold ancient historiographers to an anachronistic standard, because all historians of late antiquity were expected to elaborate on the stories they recounted, following rhetorical conventions of well-known Greek literature.

Consequently, twentieth- and twenty-first century biblical historians, using a different set of assumptions, have worked hard over the years to develop specific critical tools to sort through the Gospel traditions about Jesus and develop plausible suggestions about which stories and sayings recount historical data.

Three of the criteria these biblical historians have developed have proven particularly fruitful. Those criteria, and highly relevant examples, are detailed below.

The Criterion of Contextual Credibility

This criterion considers the historical context of a Jesus saying or story about Jesus. Is it anachronistic, or is it consistent with what we know of history? For example, it would be highly anachronistic for Jesus to tell his disciples to escalate personal conflicts to authorities in the Church (Matt. 18:15-20) when the Church hadn't even been established yet. Relevant as the instruction may have been later in the first century, in the 30s C.E. it would have made no sense.

Turning to Q, another anachronism would be the story about a Roman centurion stationed in a fishing village in Galilee. During Jesus' lifetime, there were no centurions stationed in Galilee.[2] As we'll see in Chapter Four, the story may have served an important purpose in Q and made more sense during the time of its composition, but it's unlikely that it reflects an actual encounter that Jesus had with a centurion.

As a positive example, one detail in Q that does pass the criterion of contextual credibility is the depiction of Jesus associated with John's baptismal movement. Baptismal renewal movements in Judea were common in Jesus' day, not just among John's disciples, but more famously among the Essenes of the Qumran community as well. The strong suggestion that Jesus' mission originated among just such baptismal renewal movements, which were critical of the Temple establishment and its leaders, is very plausible and fits well with what we know of the tone of Jesus' own mission.

The Criterion of Multiple Independent Attestation

This criterion hinges on the literary relationships (or, more precisely, the lack thereof) between the Gospels as described in the Introduction. The basic idea is that Jesus' sayings, and stories about Jesus, are more likely to be historically accurate if multiple texts describe those sayings and stories independently of one another. It's not just that a saying or story needs to be recorded by several sources; if a saying or story is copied by one author from another, for example, this criterion doesn't apply. The traditions need to be not only widely attested, but widely attested by independent sources, like court trial witnesses who haven't had the opportunity to compare notes.

For example, the story of Jesus calming a storm is described by three different Gospels: In Matthew 8:23-27, Mark 4:35-41, and Luke 8:22-25. However, in comparing the three stories, it's easy to notice that the authors of Matthew and Luke both copied the story from Mark. The story has multiple attestation, but not multiple *independent* attestation; it really comes from only a single known source, the Gospel of Mark.

The fact that a story (like the calming of the storm) doesn't pass this criterion doesn't automatically mean that it isn't historical; it can't prove a negative. The point rather is that this criterion can provide a plausible argument for an event having actually happened.

To cite a positive example, many different independent sources provide evidence that Jesus really did exist. The historical existence of Jesus is affirmed by the apostle Paul, the Jewish historian Josephus, and Gospels like Q, Mark, Thomas, and others writing independently of one another.[3]

Another positive example is the tradition that John the Baptizer's mission paved the way for Jesus' mission. This tradition is independently attested by Q, Mark, and John.[4] This example actually meets two of the criteria for historical accuracy, as it also met the criterion of coherence described above. Because of this, Q's description of the origins of Jesus' ministry appears plausible.

A final example is relevant to the present study: the question of whether or not Jesus was literate. Surprising as it may seem at first blush, there is no unambiguous evidence that Jesus knew how to read or write. Two stories in the New Testament Gospels suggest otherwise, but neither one passes this (or any other) criterion of historical reliability. The first is John 8:6, which describes Jesus writing something on the ground with his finger. Not only is the story not attested elsewhere; the entire passage is missing from the earliest versions of John, and is therefore likely a much later addition. The second is Luke 4:16ff, when Jesus is said to have read from the scroll of Isaiah in a synagogue in Nazareth. This passage, too, is unique; no other text describes Jesus reading from a scroll. In fact, since the vast majority of peasant Galileans were illiterate, it's highly likely that Jesus was illiterate too, as were all his disciples. The book of Acts actually says as much when it describes Peter and John as "illiterate," *agrammatoi* (literally "unlettered") in Acts 4:13.[5]

Undoubtedly Jesus knew large portions of Israel's scriptures by heart, but his lack of formal education is often cited as a significant reason that Jesus' audiences were so astonished at how knowledgeable he was, despite his ignominious origins. Here's Matthew's version of the same story which the author of Luke copied from Mark, showing how Luke alone edited Mark to add the detail about Jesus reading a scroll:

> Coming into his own country, he taught them in their synagogue. They were amazed. "Where did this man get such wisdom and mighty deeds?" they asked. "Isn't this the carpenter's son? Isn't his mother known as Mary and aren't his brothers James, Joseph, Simon, and Judas? Aren't all of his sisters around? Then where did this man get all of these

things?" They were scandalized by him (Matt. 13:54-57, DFV; cf. Mark 6:2).

John recounts the same type of reaction:

The authorities were amazed. "How can this uneducated man be so articulate?" they asked (John 7:15, DFV).[6]

Again, the criterion of multiple independent attestation can't prove a negative, so just because John 8:6 and Luke 4:16ff don't pass this criterion doesn't automatically mean that Jesus couldn't read or write. However, in the absence of compelling evidence that he did have such a formal education, it's more plausible to conclude that Jesus, like other people in his class – that is, carpenters, not scribes – simply was not literate. That would easily explain why this immensely influential teacher didn't leave behind any writings of his own, and why traditions about his teachings and activities weren't committed to ink and papyrus until years later. How much easier it would be to learn about the historical Jesus if he had been able to write an autobiography or a personal account of his own teachings!

The Criterion of Dissimilarity

This criterion, also known as "the criterion of embarrassment," works on a very different principle than the criterion of multiple independent attestation. The basic idea is that traditions which don't support the theological agendas or beliefs of Gospel authors are more likely to be accurate, since the authors are less likely to have simply made them up. Of course, this criterion doesn't automatically imply that a tradition consistent with an author's agenda should be considered suspect; after all, we should expect continuity between historical tradition and the writers who've been influenced by it. What it does mean, however, is that if a Jesus saying or a story about Jesus could be an occasion for embarrassment to a Gospel author, it's more likely to have an actual historical basis.

One pertinent example has been shown to pass both the criterion of multiple independent attestation *and* the criterion of dissimilarity; the fact that Jesus was popularly understood as a prophet.[7] N.T. Wright expands at length on the point:

> The early church is highly unlikely to have invented the many sayings, isolated but telling, scattered throughout the gospels, which call Jesus a prophet. Several of them are on his own lips. By the time the gospels were written down, the church had come to believe that Jesus was much more than a prophet. It might well have seemed risky theologically to refer to him in this way; it might have appeared that he was simply being put on a level with all the other prophets. It is therefore extremely probable that these sayings represent thoroughly authentic tradition. ... We are here, historically speaking, on certain ground.[8]

The question of just what type of leader Jesus was historically has a direct bearing on how we should evaluate the meaning and significance of Q.

Was Jesus a Rabbi or a Prophet?

Using a different type of methodology, the deeply profound Wisdom teacher Cynthia Bourgeault argues convincingly that Jesus was a Wisdom teacher.[9] After describing him in this way, however, she goes on to set that category against the category of Jesus as prophet:

> Nor was he a prophet in the usual sense of the term: a messenger sent to the people of Israel to warn them of impending political catastrophe in an attempt to redirect their hearts to God. Jesus was not interested in the political fate of Israel.[10]

But the categories of "sage" and "prophet" need not be mutually exclusive. For example, in his book cited earlier, Wright warns against playing off "the picture of Jesus as sage, a teacher of subversive wisdom," against other emphases,[11] going on to argue for "Jesus the sage" as "a subset of 'Jesus the prophet.'"[12] However, once Wright subsumes Jesus as Wisdom teacher under the category of "prophet," in actual practice the former seems conveniently to drop out of sight.

Might the truth actually be the other way around? If the reconstructed Q Gospel in its current form is any indication, it seems rather likely that Jesus' prophetic condemnation of social injustice could very well have been grounded in his subversive and counter-cultural Wisdom teaching.[13] Arland D. Jacobson states the idea succinctly in his introduction to Q in *The Complete Gospels*:

> Jesus appears in Q as a wise teacher and prophet. ... According to Q 11:49, Wisdom sent prophets to Israel. This means that in Q we have a combination of the wisdom and prophetic traditions, though this was not really new (see, e.g., Prov 1:20-33). But as a way of identifying Jesus' role, it does make Q different from the canonical gospels.[14]

Interestingly, both categories – Jesus as a Teacher of Wisdom and Jesus as a social prophet – appear evenly blended in the final passage of Jesus' first sermon in Q:

> "Why do you call me, 'Master, Master,' and don't do what I say? Everyone who hears my words and acts on them can be compared to someone building a house on bedrock. When the rain poured, and the floods came, and the winds blew and pounded that house, it didn't collapse, because it was founded on bedrock. But everyone who hears my words and doesn't act on them is like someone who built a house on the sand. When the rain poured, and the floods came, and the

winds blew and pounded that house, it collapsed immediately. How great was its fall!" (Q 6:46-49)

The idea of Jesus as a prophet of Wisdom – in short, both a popular rural sage *and* a prophetic witness against social injustice – not only satisfies critical tests of historical reliability, but also provides a plausible interpretative framework for the earliest Gospel of them all – Q.

4
The Distinctive Message of Q

The interpretation which follows builds upon what has been written so far, although at points it diverges from other interpretations of Q. These reflections should be considered provisional, and not necessarily representative of a particular consensus view.

Although Q is clearly not a narrative Gospel along the lines of Matthew, Mark, Luke, or John, read on its own terms in its reconstructed form, it does follow a logical sequence. Like the canonical Gospels, Q begins with John the Baptizer (3:2ff), followed by what may be a fragmented description of Jesus' inauguration as a Spirit-filled messenger from God (3:21, 22). A later passage in Q 7:18ff elaborates on the transition from John's mission to the arguably messianic mission of Jesus.

As in Mark, Jesus in Q appears to be anointed as God's Son when the Spirit rests upon him at his baptism (cf. Mark 1:10, 11). This anointing may be interpreted as messianic in some sense — that is, within the tradition of the Davidic messiah as God's Son — although strongly reinterpreted in the temptation story which immediately follows, wherein Jesus repeatedly resists the temptation to fight for political domination over others (Q 4:1-13). Jesus' filial relationship to God is one that his followers can apparently share by trusting in God's provision (11:2) and abandoning themselves to the care of the holy Spirit (12:12).

The temptation story is immediately followed by Jesus' first sermon, a lengthy monologue in the venerable Wisdom tradition of the "Two Ways" (6:20ff).[1] The sermon, arguably Jesus' core teaching (forming the basis of Matthew's "Sermon on the Mount" and Luke's "Sermon on the Plain"), emphasizes radical grace, mercy, and transformative love, even for enemies.

These traditional Wisdom teachings reoccur throughout Q, as in 10:21ff and 12:35ff. Interspersed with these teachings are equally earnest warnings against disregarding the path of Wisdom, as in 11:29ff. Teachings about the coming of God's true reign (cf. 17:20ff), and the true way to enter that divine reign (cf. 13:24ff), are prominent throughout.

Jesus' addressees in Q appear to be his followers in Galilee; references to Nazareth (4:16), Capernaum (7:2; 10:15), and Bethsaida (10:13) bear this out. The immediate mission of Jesus, and by extension his followers, is to the surrounding rural villages (10:2ff), not people from other nations, the "Gentiles," who are not generally portrayed in a positive light (cf. 6:34; 12:30). The two exceptions, in 7:1ff and 13:29, appear to function more as critical rhetorical techniques than as precursors of a Gentile mission.[2] Indeed, the unusual story of the Roman centurion in Capernaum makes particular sense closer to the time of the Jewish-Roman war. The story is clearly anachronistic since Roman centurions weren't present in Galilee in Jesus' time.[3] But the commendation of the trusting outsider in contrast to local leaders underscores the warning of rejecting the Wisdom path.

Finally, in the concluding passage of the extant portion of Q, Jesus describes his followers as carrying on his tradition in leadership positions in 22:30.

Consequently, Q seems to articulate a different view than Mark on the question of Jesus' legitimate successors. The author of Mark clearly downplays the credibility of Jesus' disciples, possibly in favor of Paul's leadership.[4] In response, the author of Matthew appears to have taken over the narrative of Mark and subverted it, in part by incorporating the Wisdom tradition and pro-disciple leadership described in Q and in part by adding comments about the organization of the Church (cf. Matt. 18:15-20), founded on Peter and the disciples (cf. Matt. 16:17-19). Similarly, Luke seems to have created a synthesis by combining Mark and Q and crafting a Church history in Acts that incorporates Paul's mission, but subordinates Paul to the Jerusalem church.

If this thesis is plausible, it suggests not only commonality between some of the earliest Gospel authors and their communities, but tension as well, particularly with respect to questions about legitimate spiritual authority among Jesus' followers.[5] This tension is more pronounced in other Gospels, such as Mary[6] and Judas.[7]

It also suggests that different portraits of Jesus and his mission are necessary to capture the fullness of his multi-faceted truth.[8] Far from settling all the questions about Jesus and what he still has to teach us today, increased scrutiny of these diverse Gospels promises to open up the flood-gates and pave the way for more incredible revelations to come.

5
Q and the Wisdom Tradition

Among other things, the previous chapter affirmed the distinctive message of Q with respect to the "Two Ways" teaching of the Wisdom tradition. This point should be elaborated, especially as it pertains to spiritual teachings and practices.

The Wisdom tradition has a venerable and cosmopolitan history. It isn't limited to the religions of Judaism and Christianity. This tradition emphasizes "praxis" over belief, spiritual reflection over dogma.

Significantly, the New Testament frequently describes Jesus' movement not as a "religion" per se but rather, much more descriptively, as "the Way."[1] Considering the broad diversity of equally valid Christian traditions,[2] we may regard the Way as a journey of growth toward spiritual maturity, not a forced march to the beat of a conformist drum of systematic doctrinal belief systems that define who is "in" and who is "out" of the chosen people's boundaries. Those who are "born again" in the words of the New Testament aren't spiritually birthed as fully mature individuals, but as spiritually awakened infants who can look forward to a lifetime of divine awe and discovery.

Q itself does not require adherence to a set of beliefs or abstract teachings about the "person" of Christ or "Christian" dogma. Rather, it calls women and men to the radical path of Wisdom, the very practical, down-to-earth, counter-cultural journey of spiritual transformation. As the Rev. Cynthia Bourgeault describes it:

You will find the "practice" part of the Wisdom tradition
still at the base of all the great world religions. It's remarkable
how, no matter which spiritual path you pursue, the nuts and
bolts of transformation wind up looking pretty much the
same: surrender, detachment, compassion, forgiveness.
Whether you're a Christian, a Buddhist, a Jew, a Sufi, or a
sannyasin, you will still go through the same eye of the needle
to get to where your true heart lies. But the *meaning* accorded
to this spiritual passage varies widely among the traditions ...
no single tradition preserves the whole of the original
Wisdom cosmology.[3]

Put differently, the Wisdom tradition has a long history in
each of the world's major historic religions. Mahayana Buddhism,
Jewish Kabbalah, Christian Mysticism, Islamic Sufism, and similar
traditions (both ancient and modern) drink deeply from the same
well of contemplative spirituality, and faithful travelers of these
diverse Ways often speak the same type of language.

This does not mean, as some are inclined to think, that all the
world's religions can be collapsed into a single system, or that the
core essence of each can be reduced to a single common
denominator. Every world religion is unique; any attempt to
conflate them inevitably results in a smorgasbord of cherry-
picked doctrines. In the West, that usually looks like an individual-
oriented religion with a generic commitment to neighborly love.
But this sausage-grinding type of religious ideology doesn't
faithfully represent the uniqueness of very distinct traditions,
which should not be homogenized or confused.

Those who (like myself) were born and raised as Christians
need not reinvent religion in order to discover the Wisdom path
of spiritual transformation. Like other traditions, Christianity
preserves its own treasure trove of contemplative and
transformative spiritual practices. These include *lectio divina* and
centering prayer,[4] among others – practical exercises in releasing

ourselves from the grip of anxiety and limitation, and welcoming the indwelling of divinity.

As Bourgeault describes it, Jesus' own Wisdom teaching was not a doctrine of ascetic renunciation, but rather an invitation to reckless self-abandon to love.[5] Jesus modeled a life of faithful surrender to the unpredictable movement of the divine Spirit.

Jesus himself described this more vividly by proclaiming "God's reign," something that may not be easy to grasp.[6] What is "God's reign"? Q doesn't define it, but does describe it in terms of the direct presence of the divine. Its coming is to be prayed for (11:2), and it's to be sought after (12:31). It can be compared to the growth of an impressive tree (13:18, 19) and to the fermenting of yeast hidden in flour (13:20, 21). Its coming won't be observed by the naked eye; rather, it's to be recognized as already present (17:20, 21). Divine healing is evidence of its arrival (10:9; 11:20). It's a new reality arriving on the heels of John's mission (7:28), but it's under attack (16:16) and kept from the people by lawyers (11:52). Its central paradox is that in reality it belongs to "the last" (13:28-30) and those who are poor (6:20) – those who are disenfranchised, marginalized, or excluded.

Paradox is an integral aspect both of Q and of the Wisdom path generally. In this spiritual tradition, we receive by letting go: "Whoever exalts themselves will be humbled, and whoever humbles themselves will be exalted" (14:11; cp. 17:33). When we empty ourselves, we're filled, and become more conscious of our connection with the divine. Jesus recognized his own divine origins, and summoned others to follow him on Wisdom's spiritual path of divine self-discovery.

In two Q passages, Jesus describes this spiritual perception using the metaphor of the human eye (6:39-42; 11:34). Over a thousand years later, another famous mystic, Meister Eckhart, wrote eloquently about our perception of the divine in a similar way: "The eye with which I see God is the same eye with which God sees me: my eye and God's eye are one eye, one seeing, one knowing and one love."[7] This is "unitive" consciousness, described in various ways by different traditions. For example, describing the perspective of Jewish Kabbalah, Daniel C. Matt writes that "there is a higher level, a deeper realm ... at the ultimate stage the kabbalist no longer differentiates one thing from another. Conceptual thought, with all its distinctions and connections, dissolves."[8]

The fact that unitive consciousness transcends "conceptual thought" highlights the irony that revelations conceal as much as they reveal. Should there be any doubt about this, just consider the cryptic language of the Book of "Revelation." Despite its mysterious imagery, however, one passage in Revelation vividly depicts the paradox of enlightenment: When the seventh and final seal is opened on the divine scroll, the visionary describes nothing except silence in heaven (8:1).

For most of us, these contemplative moments of experiencing the divine, generally in visions or during meditation, are few and far between. We are physically embodied in a world of binary perception that must be navigated on a day-to-day basis. No one would want to drive a car while experiencing unitive consciousness. The point of seeking the divine isn't to escape the world, but to be transformed so that we can live more fully in the world.

Consequently, "spiritual" does not necessarily mean "ahistorical" or anti-social.[9] "God's reign" purifies and transforms inner perception, but it also confronts social injustice (cf. 11:42) and drives out evil – the "demonic."

The spiritual conflict between the divine and the "demonic" is most vividly described in Q 11:14-26. How may we understand these "demonic" forces in a contemporary post-enlightenment context? The ancient depiction of spiritual forces as personal beings (as in Q) challenges contemporary readers to consider this question. Are the "demons" of ancient literature mythical, metaphorical, or metaphysical? And if they really exist, what are they?

In a telling description, the "demon" which Jesus "was casting out" in Q 11:14 was named for the malady which it caused. Specifically, the "demon that couldn't speak" needed to be expelled from "the person who couldn't speak." In other words, the "demon" that afflicted its victim was identified in terms of its physical manifestation.

Though it would be anachronistic to argue that Q's ancient author shared this understanding, we may nevertheless consider the explanation of a contemporary Jewish mystic, Rabbi David A. Cooper:

> In physical reality, every move we make is dependent upon electromagnetic energy. In the metaphysical realm, rather than call this energy electromagnetic, we could call it angelic-demonic. Every move we make is supported by an angel or demon. Moreover, everything we do creates new angels and demons. They represent lines of force, packets of energy like light photons, neither wave nor particle, and they cannot be distinguished except through results. The metaphysical magnets associated with the God realms are called angels, and those with the satanic realms are called demons.[10]

So we may not need to think of "angels" and "demons" as disembodied personalities with self-determination, will, and consciousness. We may just as well think of them as impersonal cosmic energies with positive and negative impacts on our lives.

In proclaiming "God's reign" and calling his followers to do likewise, as in Q 10:9, Jesus addressed the suffering and brokenness among countless people struggling to survive in difficult circumstances. The simple (but not easy) path of the Wisdom tradition, universally accessible to everyone, addresses the most basic of human needs (cf. Q 11:2-13).

Appendix
The Gospel of Q:
A Literal Translation

The translation of Q presented in this Appendix has been committed to the public domain. It may be freely copied and used, in whole or in part, changed or unchanged, for any purpose. The text is based on the reconstruction of James M. Robinson, Paul Hoffman, and John S., Kloppenborg, eds., *The Critical Edition of Q: Synopsis including the Gospels of Matthew and Luke, Mark and Thomas with English, German, and French Translations of Q and Thomas* (Peeters), 2000. *The Critical Edition* represents probably the most refined and detailed work on Q to date; it meticulously sorts through the "double tradition" of Matthew and Luke word-for-word, considering the respective editorial tendencies of both Gospels in carefully considering the probable wording of the original source shared between the two.

Q (from *Quelle*, meaning "source") is widely believed to have been written in Greek, probably in Galilee sometime between 50 and 70 C.E.

What follows is a more literal translation than the one presented in Chapter Two. For a description of the differences between the two, see Chapter One.

Gaps in the reconstructed text are denoted by square brackets. These represent unknown portions of the text that can't be reconstructed.

QLk 3:2 John […] ³[…] the entire region around the Jordan […]

⁷He told the crowds who went out to be baptized, "You offspring of vipers, who warned you to flee from the fury to come? ⁸So bear fruit worthy of change! Don't start to say to yourselves, 'We have Abraham for our ancestor,' because I tell you that God is able to raise up children for Abraham from these stones.

⁹"Even now the axe lies at the root of the trees! So every tree that doesn't bear good fruit is cut down and thrown into the fire.

¹⁶"I baptize you in water, but one who's greater than I will come, the thong of whose sandals I'm not worthy to loosen. He'll baptize you in holy Spirit and fire. ¹⁷His pitchfork is in his hand to clean out his threshing floor, and to gather the wheat into his barn; but he'll burn up the chaff with a fire that can't be put out."

²¹[…] Jesus […] baptized […] heaven opened ²²and […] the Spirit […] on him […] Son […]

4:1 Jesus was led by the Spirit into the desert ²to be tested by the devil. He didn't eat anything for forty days […] he was hungry.

³And the devil told him, "If you're God's Son, tell these stones to turn into bread."

⁴And Jesus replied, "It's written, 'A person shouldn't live on bread alone.'"

⁹The devil led him to Jerusalem, set him on the pinnacle of the temple, and said, "If you're God's Son, throw yourself down, ¹⁰because it's written, 'God will put God's angels in charge of you,' ¹¹and 'On their hands they'll bear you up, so that you don't dash your foot against a stone.'"

¹²And in reply Jesus told him, "It's been said, 'Don't test the Lord, your God.'"

⁵Then the devil took him to a very high mountain and showed him all the empires of the world and their glory and told him, ⁶"I'll give you all these, ⁷if you'll bow to me."

⁸And in reply Jesus told him, "It's written: 'Bow to the Lord your God, and serve God only.'"

¹³And the devil left him.

¹⁶[...] Nazareth [...]
6:20 He looked up at his disciples and said:

> Blessed are you who are poor,
> because yours is God's reign.
>
> ²¹Blessed are you who are hungry,
> because you'll be full.
>
> Blessed are you who mourn,
> because you'll be comforted.

²²"Blessed are you when they criticize you, persecute you, and spread lies about you because of the Son of Humanity. ²³Rejoice and be glad, because your heavenly reward is great; for that's how they persecuted the prophets before you.

²⁷"Love your enemies, ²⁸and pray for those who persecute you. ³⁵You'll become children of your Father, who makes the sun rise on those who are evil and those who are good, and sends rain on those who are just and those who are unjust.

²⁹"When someone slaps you on the cheek, offer the other one too. When someone sues you for your shirt, give them your coat too. ^QMt 5:41^When someone makes you go one mile, go an extra mile. ^QLk 6:30^Give to everyone who asks you, and when someone borrows your things, don't ask for them back.

³¹"Treat people how you want them to treat you. ³²If you love those who love you, why should you be rewarded? Don't even toll collectors do that? ³⁴And if you lend to those from whom you expect repayment, why should you be rewarded? Don't even gentiles do that? ³⁶Be merciful, just like your Father.

³⁷"Don't judge, and you won't be judged; ^QMt 7:2^because you'll be judged the way that you judge. ^QLk 6:38^And you'll be measured the way that you measure.

³⁹"Can someone who can't see guide another person who can't see? Won't they both fall into a pit? ⁴⁰A disciple isn't greater

than their teacher. It's enough for the disciple to become like their teacher.

[41]"Why do you see the speck that's in your brother's eye, but don't consider the beam that's in your own eye? [42]How can you tell your brother, 'Let me get that speck out of your eye,' when you don't see the beam that's in your own eye? You hypocrite! First get the beam out of your own eye, and then you'll see clearly to get the speck out of your brother's eye.

[43]"No good tree bears rotten fruit, nor does a rotten tree bear good fruit. [44]Every tree is known by its own fruit. Are figs gathered from thorns, or grapes from thistles? [45]The person who's good brings good things out of their good treasure, and the person who's evil brings evil things out of evil treasure, because one's mouth speaks from the overflow of the heart.

[46]"Why do you call me, 'Master, Master,' and don't do what I say? [47]Everyone who hears my words and acts on them [48]can be compared to someone building a house on bedrock. When the rain poured, and the floods came, and the winds blew and pounded that house, it didn't collapse, because it was founded on bedrock. [49]But everyone who hears my words and doesn't act on them is like someone who built a house on the sand. When the rain poured, and the floods came, and the winds blew and pounded that house, it collapsed immediately. How great was its fall!"

7:1 And so when it happened that he had finished saying these things, he went to Capernaum. [3]A centurion approached and begged him and said, "My boy is sick."

And Jesus told him, "I'll go heal him."

[6]And the centurion replied, "Master, I'm not worthy for you to come under my roof. [7]Just say the word, and my boy will be healed. [8]I'm also in a chain of command, with soldiers under me. I tell one, 'Go,' and they go; I tell another, 'Come,' and they come; I tell my servant, 'Do this,' and they do it."

[9]Jesus was amazed when he heard this. He told his followers, "I'm telling you the truth: I haven't found such trust even in Israel."

¹⁸When John heard all these things, he sent his disciples ¹⁹to ask him, "Are you the coming one, or should we look for someone else?"

²²And he replied to them, "Go and tell John what you've heard and seen. Those who:

> are blind, regain their sight;
> have challenges of mobility, walk;
> have leprosy, are cured;
> are deaf, hear;
> are dead, are raised up;
> are poor, have good news announced to them.

²³Blessed is the one who isn't scandalized by me."

²⁴And when they had left, he started to talk to the crowds about John. "What did you go out into the desert to see? A reed shaken by the wind? ²⁵Then what did you go out to see? A man wearing fancy clothes? Look, those who wear fancy clothes live in palaces. ²⁶Then what did you go out to see? A prophet? Yes, I'm telling you, and much more than a prophet, ²⁷because it's written about him:

> Look, I'm sending my messenger ahead of you,
> who'll prepare your path for you.

²⁸"I'm telling you that John is greater than anyone who's been born, but whoever is least in God's reign is still greater than he, ²⁹because John came to you [...] the toll collectors and [...] ³⁰but [...] him.

³¹"To what, then, can I compare this generation? What's it like? ³²It's like children sitting in the marketplaces calling to each other:

> We played the flute for you,
> but you didn't dance.
> We mourned,

But you didn't weep.

[33]"John didn't come eating or drinking, and you say, 'He's demonized!' [34]The Son of Humanity has come eating and drinking, and you say, 'Look, a glutton and a drunk, a friend of toll collectors and outsiders!' [35]But Wisdom is vindicated by her children."

9:57 And someone told him, "I'll follow you wherever you go."

[58]And Jesus told him, "Foxes have holes and birds of the sky have nests, but the Son of Humanity has nowhere to rest his head."

[59]But someone else told him, "Master, let me go and bury my father first."

[60]But he told him, "Follow me, and let the dead bury their own dead."

10:2 He told his disciples, "The harvest is plentiful, but the workers are few. So ask the Lord of the harvest to send workers into the fields. [3]Go! Look, I send you out like lambs among wolves. [4]Don't carry a purse, bag, sandals, or staff. Don't greet anyone on the road. [5]Whenever you enter a house, first say, 'Peace to this house.' [6]If a peaceful person is there, let your blessing rest on them; but if not, take back your blessing. [7]Stay in the same house, eating and drinking whatever they give you, because the worker is worthy of their wages. Don't move around from house to house. [8]If they welcome you in whatever town you enter, eat whatever is set before you. [9]Heal those who are sick there and tell them, 'God's reign is at hand!' [10]But if they don't welcome you in whatever town you enter, when you're leaving that town, [11]shake the dust from your feet. [12]I'm telling you that on that day, it'll be better for Sodom than for that town!

[13]"Woe to you, Chorazin! Woe to you, Bethsaida! If the great deeds done in your midst had been done in Tyre and Sidon, they would have changed a long time ago in sackcloth and ashes. [14]But it will be better for Tyre and Sidon than for you in the judgment!

¹⁵And you, Capernaum, you don't think you'll be exalted to heaven, do you? You'll fall down to Hades!

¹⁶"Whoever welcomes you welcomes me, and whoever welcomes me welcomes the one who sent me."

²¹Then he said, "Thank you, Father, Lord of heaven and earth, for hiding these things from the wise and learned and revealing them to children. Yes, Father, this was what you wanted. ²²My Father has given me everything. No one knows who the son is except the Father, or who the Father is except the son, and the one to whom the son wants to reveal him.

²³"Blessed are the eyes that see what you see. ²⁴I'm telling you that many prophets and rulers wanted to see what you see, but didn't see it; and to hear what you hear, but didn't hear it.

11:2 "When you pray, say:

> Father,
> We honor your holy name.
> Let your reign come.
> ³Give us our daily bread today.
> ⁴Forgive us our debts,
> because we too forgive everyone who's indebted to us.
> Don't put us in harm's way.

⁹"I'm telling you, ask and you'll receive. Look and you'll find. Knock and it'll be opened for you, ¹⁰because everyone who asks receives. The one who looks finds. To one who knocks it'll be opened. ¹¹Which of you would give your child a stone if they ask for bread? ¹²Or who would give them a snake if they ask for fish? ¹³So if you, evil as you are, know how to give good gifts to your children, how much more will the heavenly Father give good things to those who ask!"

¹⁴He was casting out a demon that couldn't speak. And when the demon came out, the person who couldn't speak started talking. And the crowds were amazed. ¹⁵But some said, "He casts out demons with the power of Beelzebul, the ruler of the demons!"

¹⁷Knowing what they were thinking, he told them, "Every divided empire is devastated, and a divided house will fall. ¹⁸If the Enemy is divided, how will its empire endure? ¹⁹But if Beelzebul gives me power to cast out demons, who gives your people power to cast them out? So they prove you wrong. ²⁰But if I cast out demons by the finger of God, then God's reign has come to you!

²³"Whoever isn't with me is against me, and whoever doesn't gather with me, scatters. ²⁴When the impure spirit leaves someone, it journeys through arid places looking for rest, but doesn't find it. Then it says, 'I'll return to the home I left'; ²⁵and when it comes back, it finds it swept and organized. ²⁶Then it goes out and brings seven other spirits that are even more evil, and they move in and live there. That person ends up even worse off than before."

¹⁶Some demanded him to show a sign. ²⁹But he said, "This is an evil generation. It demands a sign, but no sign will be provided except the sign of Jonah! ³⁰As Jonah became a sign to the Ninevites, so the Son of Humanity will be a sign to this generation. ³¹The queen of the South will rise up in the judgment with this generation and will condemn it, because she came from the ends of the earth to hear Solomon's wisdom; and look, something greater than Solomon is here. ³²The people of Nineveh will rise up in the judgment with this generation and will condemn it, because they changed in response to Jonah's announcement, and look, something greater than Jonah is here.

³³"No one lights a lamp and hides it, but puts it on a lampstand, and it enlightens everyone in the house. ³⁴Your eye is the body's lamp. If your eye is single, your whole body is full of light. If your eye is evil, your whole body is dark. ³⁵So if the light within you is dark, how dark it is!

⁴²"Woe to you, Pharisees! You tithe your mint, dill, and cumin, but you ignore justice, mercy, and trust. You should've done these without ignoring the others.

³⁹"Woe to you, Pharisees! You clean the outside of the cup and dish, but inside they're full of greed and decadence. ⁴¹Clean the inside of the cup, and its outside will be clean too.

⁴³"Woe to you, Pharisees! You love the place of honor at banquets, the front seat in the synagogues, and accolades in the marketplaces. ⁴⁴Woe to you, because you're like unmarked graves that people walk on without knowing it.

⁴⁶"And woe to you, lawyers! You load people with burdens that are hard to bear, but you yourselves won't even lift a finger to help them.

⁵²"Woe to you, lawyers! You shut people out of God's reign. You didn't enter, and didn't let those enter who are trying to do so.

⁴⁷"Woe to you, because you build the tombs of the prophets whom your ancestors killed. ⁴⁸You prove that you're the descendants of your ancestors. ⁴⁹So Wisdom said, 'I'll send prophets and sages. Some of them they'll kill and persecute.' ⁵⁰So this generation will be guilty of the blood of all the prophets shed from the beginning of the world, ⁵¹from the blood of Abel to the blood of Zechariah, who died between the altar and the sanctuary. Yes, I'm telling you that this generation will be held responsible.

12:2 "Nothing is concealed that won't be revealed, nor hidden that won't be made known. ³Whatever I tell you in the dark, say in the light; and whatever you hear whispered in your ear, announce from the housetops.

⁴"Don't be afraid of those who kill the body but can't kill the soul. ⁵Instead, fear the one who can kill both the soul and the body in Gehenna.

⁶"Don't five sparrows cost two pennies? Yet not one of them will fall to the ground without your Father's permission. ⁷Even the hairs of your head are all numbered. Don't be afraid, because you're more valuable than many sparrows.

⁸"Everyone who publicly acknowledges me, the Son of Humanity will acknowledge in front of the angels. ⁹But whoever publicly denies me will be denied in front of the angels. ¹⁰Whoever speaks out against the Son of Humanity will be forgiven, but whoever speaks out against the holy Spirit won't be forgiven. ¹¹When they bring you before the synagogues, don't

worry about how or what you should say, [12]because the holy Spirit will teach you at that time what you should say.

[33]"Don't store treasures for yourselves here on earth, where moth and rust destroy and robbers break in and steal. Instead, store treasures for yourselves in heaven, where neither moth nor rust destroy and where robbers don't break in or steal. [34]Because where your treasure is, there your heart will be too.

[22]"So I'm telling you not to worry about your life, about what you'll eat; or about your body, what you'll wear. [23]Isn't life more than food, and the body more than clothes? [24]Think about how the ravens don't sow, reap, or gather into barns, yet God feeds them. Aren't you more valuable than the birds?

[25]"Which of you can grow any taller by worrying? [26]And why worry about clothes? [27]Look at how the lilies grow. They don't work or spin, yet I'm telling you that even Solomon in all his glory wasn't dressed like one of these. [28]But if God clothes the grass of the field, which is here today and is thrown into the oven tomorrow, won't God clothe you even more, you who have little trust? [29]So don't worry. Don't ask, 'What are we going to eat?' or 'What are going to drink?' or 'What are we going to wear?' [30]The gentiles look for all these things, but your Father knows that you need all of them. [31]Instead, look for God's reign, and all these things will be given to you too.

[39]"But know this: If the master of the house had known at what time the robber was coming, he wouldn't have let his house be broken into. [40]You too should be ready, because the Son of Humanity is coming when you don't expect it.

[42]"Then who is the trustworthy and wise servant who was entrusted by their master to hand out rations to the household at the right time? [43]Blessed is that servant whose master finds them doing so when he comes. [44]I'm telling you the truth: he'll put them in charge of all that he owns. [45]But if that servant says in their heart, 'My master is late,' and starts to beat the other servants and to eat and drink with those who are addicted to alcohol, [46]the master of that servant will come when they don't expect it, at a

time that they don't know, and will rip them to shreds and throw them out with those who are untrustworthy.

[49]"I came to cast fire on the earth, and how I wish it were already kindled! [51]Do you think that I came to bring peace on earth? I didn't come to bring peace, but a sword! [53]Because I've come:

> [53]To pit son against father,
> daughter against her mother,
> daughter-in-law against her mother-in-law."

[54]He told them, "When it's evening, you say, 'There'll be good weather, because the sky is red.' [55]In the morning, 'There'll be wintry weather today, because the sky is red and threatening.' [56]You know how to interpret the appearance of the sky. Why don't you know how to interpret the time?

[58]"When you're going with your adversary, do your best to settle the case on the way there, or else your adversary may hand you over to the judge, and the judge to the officer, and the officer may throw you into prison. [59]I'm telling you that you won't get out of there until you've paid the very last penny!

13:18 "What is God's reign like, and to what should I compare it? [19]It can be compared to a mustard seed which someone sowed in their garden. It grew and became a tree, and the birds of the sky nested in its branches."

[20]"And again: To what should I compare God's reign? [21]It can be compared to yeast which a woman hid in fifty pounds of flour until it was all fermented.

[24]"Enter through the narrow door, because many will try to enter, though only a few will succeed. [25]When the master of the house gets up and locks the door, you'll be standing outside and knocking on it, saying, 'Master, open up for us!'

"But he'll reply, 'I don't know you.'

[26]"Then you'll start saying, 'We ate and drank with you, and you taught in our streets.'

²⁷"But he'll tell you, 'I don't know you. Get away from me, you criminals!'

²⁹"Many will come from east and west and dine ²⁸with Abraham, Isaac, and Jacob in God's reign, but you'll be thrown out into the outer darkness, where there'll be weeping and grinding of teeth. ³⁰Those who are last will be first, and those who are first will be last.

³⁴"Jerusalem, Jerusalem, who kills the prophets and stones those who are sent to her! How often I would've gathered your children together, like a hen gathers her chicks under her wings, but you wouldn't let me! ³⁵Look, your house is left abandoned. I'm telling you that you won't see me until the time comes when you say, 'Blessed is the one who comes in the name of the Lord!'

14:11 "Whoever exalts themselves will be humbled, and whoever humbles themselves will be exalted.

¹⁶"Someone planning a great dinner invited many guests. ¹⁷When dinner was ready, they sent their servant to tell the invited guests, 'Come, because it's ready now!'

¹⁸"One excused himself because of his farm. ¹⁹Another excused himself because of his business. ²¹The servant went back and told their master all this. Then the master of the house became angry and told the servant, ²³'Go out to the highways and urge people to come in so that my house may be filled.'

²⁶"Whoever doesn't hate father and mother can't be my disciple, and whoever doesn't hate son and daughter can't be my disciple. ²⁷Whoever doesn't carry their own cross and follow me can't be my disciple.

17:33 "Whoever tries to find their life will lose it, but whoever loses their life for my sake will find it.

14:34 "Salt is good, but if it's lost its flavor, how can you get it back? ³⁵It's no good for the soil or the manure pile. It's thrown away.

16:13 "No one can follow two masters, because they'll either hate one and love the other, or they'll be devoted to one and despise the other. You can't serve both God and Mammon.

¹⁶"The Torah and the prophets were announced until John. Since then, God's reign has been violated, and the violent plunder it. ¹⁷But it's easier for heaven and earth to disappear than for one smallest letter or one tiny pen stroke to drop out of the Torah.

¹⁸"Everyone who divorces his wife and remarries is unfaithful to her, and whoever marries someone who's divorced is unfaithful too.

17:1 "There's no way that people won't be tripped up, but woe to the one who causes it! ²It'd be better for them if a millstone were hung around their neck and they were thrown into the sea, than for them to trip up one of these little ones.

15:4 "Which of you, if you had a hundred sheep and lost one of them, wouldn't leave the ninety-nine in the hills and go after the one that got lost? ⁵When they find it, ⁷I'm telling you that they'll rejoice over it more than over the ninety-nine that didn't wander off.

⁸"Or what woman with ten silver coins, if she loses one, wouldn't light a lamp, sweep the house, and look everywhere until she found it? ⁹When she finds it, she calls together her friends and neighbors and says, 'Rejoice with me, because I've found the coin that I'd lost!' ¹⁰In the same way, I'm telling you, the angels rejoice over one wrongdoer who changes.

17:3 "If your brother offends you, correct him. If he changes, forgive him. ⁴Even if he offends you seven times a day, then forgive him seven times.

⁶"If you had trust as big as a mustard seed, you could tell this mulberry tree, 'Be uprooted and be planted in the sea,' and it would obey you."

²⁰When he was asked when God's reign would come, he replied to them, "The coming of God's reign can't be observed. ²¹Nor will they say, 'Look over here!' or 'Look over there!' Because look, God's reign is among you.

²³"If they tell you, 'Look, he's in the desert!' don't go out; or 'Look, he's inside,' don't follow, ²⁴because as the lightning flashes in the east and is seen in the west, so will the Son of Humanity be in his day. ³⁷Where there's a corpse, there the vultures will gather.

²⁶"As it was in the days of Noah, so it will be in the day of the Son of Humanity. ²⁷In those days they were eating and drinking, marrying and giving in marriage, until the day that Noah entered the ark, and the flood came and swept all of them away. ³⁰That's what it will be like on the day the Son of Humanity is revealed.

³⁴"I'm telling you, there'll be two men in the field; one will be taken and the other will be left. ³⁵There'll be two women grinding at the mill; one will be taken and the other will be left.

19:12 "A certain person went on a trip. ¹³He called ten of his servants, gave them ten minas, and told them, 'Do business with this until I return.'

¹⁵"After a long time the master of those servants returned to settle accounts with them. ¹⁶The first one came and said, 'Master, your mina has made ten more minas.'

¹⁷"He told him, 'Well done, good servant! Since you've been trustworthy with a little, I'll put you in charge of much.'

¹⁸"The second came and said, 'Master, Your mina has made five minas.'

¹⁹"He told him, 'Well done, good servant! Since you've been trustworthy with a little, I'll put you in charge of much.'

²⁰"The other came and said, 'Master, ²¹I know you're a strict man, reaping where you didn't sow and gathering where you didn't scatter. I went out and hid your mina in the ground. Look, here's what belongs to you!'

²²"He told him, 'You evil servant! You knew that I reap what I didn't sow and gather where I didn't scatter? ²³ So why didn't you invest my money with the bankers? Then when I returned, I would've gotten it back, with interest. ²⁴So take the mina away from him and give it to the one who has ten minas, ²⁶because everyone who has will be given more, but whoever doesn't have will lose even what little they do have.'

22:28 "You who've followed me ³⁰will sit on thrones, judging the twelve tribes of Israel."

Notes

Introduction

[1]For this, and what follows, cf. Mark M. Mattison, *The Gospel of Judas: The Sarcastic Gospel* (CreateSpace Independent Publishing Platform), 2014, pp. 7-8.

[2]Cf. Marcus Borg, *The Lost Gospel Q: The Original Sayings of Jesus* (Ulysses Press), 1996, p. 26.

[3]For this, and what follows, cf. Mark M. Mattison, *The Gospel of Thomas: A New Translation for Spiritual Seekers* (CreateSpace Independent Publishing Platform), pp. 16, 17.

Chapter One

[1]John S. Kloppenborg, *The Formation of Q: Trajectories in Ancient Wisdom Collections* (Fortress), 1987.

[2]Cf. Borg, *op. cit.*, p. 16: "But many scholars are skeptical that Q can be divided into successive layers of development. The issue is not whether Q was a developing tradition; clearly it was, just as the Gospels as a whole are the product of the developing traditions of early Christian movements. The issue, rather, is whether Q can be neatly divided into a series of discernable and discrete stages of development."

[3]N.T. Wright, *The New Testament and the People of God* (Fortress), 1992, pp. 435-443.

[4]*Ibid.*, pp. 438, 439.

[5]Cf. Mattison, *Thomas*, pp. 10-12.

[6]*Ibid.*, pp. 12-14.

[7]Wright, *op. cit.*, p. 441.

[8]Cf. John S. Kloppenborg, "On Dispensing with Q? Goodacre on the Relation of Luke to Matthew," *New Testament Studies*, 2003, Vol. 49, pp. 210-236.

[9]James M. Robinson, Paul Hoffman, and John S., Kloppenborg, eds., *The Critical Edition of Q: Synopsis including the Gospels of Matthew and Luke, Mark and Thomas with English, German, and French Translations of Q and Thomas* (Peeters), 2000.

[10]Cf. Wright, *op. cit.*, p. 441.

[11]It should also be noted that Q doesn't deny the crucifixion either; cf. Q 14:27.

[12]In my colloquial translation of Thomas, I used the word "Source" as a more descriptive and comprehensive alternative to "Father." For this translation, however, the image of a caring parent (Provider) seems to best capture the nuance of the "Father" metaphor in Q.

Chapter Three

[1]Cf. Robert Orlando, *Apostle Paul: A Polite Bribe* (Cascade Books), 2014, pp. 1, 2.

[2]Cf. Arland D. Jacobson, "Sayings Gospel Q," in Robert J. Miller, ed., *The Complete Gospels: Fourth Edition* (Polebridge Press), 2010, p. 266.

[3]Cf. Bart Ehrman, *The Historical Jesus: Part I* (The Teaching Company), 2000, p. 43.

[4]*Ibid.*, p. 46.

[5]Most Bible translations render the term simply as "uneducated."

[6]Cf. also Matt. 22:33; Mark 11:18.

[7]Cf. William R. Herzog II, *Jesus, Justice, and the Reign of God: A Ministry of Liberation* (Westminster John Knox Press), 2000, pp. 47-49.

[8]N.T. Wright, *Jesus and the Victory of God* (Fortress), 1996, pp. 162, 168.

[9]Cf. Cynthia Bourgeault, *The Wisdom Jesus: Transforming Heart and Mind – a New Perspective on Christ and His Message* (Shambhala), 2008, pp. 24, 25.

[10]*Ibid.*, p. 25.

[11]Wright, *Jesus*, p. 311.

[12]*Ibid.*, p. 314.

[13]Marcus Borg articulates just such a perspective in his later book *Jesus: Uncovering the Life, Teachings, and Relevance of a Religious Revolutionary* (HarperSanFrancisco), 2006, describing Jesus both as "Teacher of an Enlightened Wisdom" (pp. 130, 131) and as "Prophet" (p. 131), as well as a Jewish spirit-filled mystic (pp. 131-135).

[14]Arland, *op. cit.*, pp. 258, 259.

Chapter Four

[1]Cf. Borg, *Q,* pp. 17, 18.

[2]Cf. William Arnal, "The Q Document," in Matt Jackson-McCabe, ed., *Jewish Christianity Reconsidered: Rethinking Ancient Groups and Texts* (Fortress), 2007, p. 142: "Q's positive references to Gentiles are not reflections of an actual Gentile constituent in their group, nor awareness of any real 'Gentile mission,' but are rather *shaming* devices, rhetorical techniques for underscoring the criticism directed at Israel."

[3]Cf. Chapter Three, Note 2, above.

[4]Cf. April D. DeConick, *The Thirteenth Apostle: What the Gospel of Judas Really Says* (Continuum), 2007, rev. ed. 2009, pp. 111-114.

[5]On models of church authority, cf. Mattison, *Judas*, p. 47.

[6]Cf. Mark M. Mattison, *The Gospel of Mary: A Fresh Translation and Holistic Approach* (CreateSpace Independent Publishing Platform), 2013, pp. 46-48.

[7]Cf. Mattison, *Judas*, pp. 20-23.

[8]Cf. Jean Yves-Leloup, *Judas and Jesus: Two Faces of a Single Revelation* Inner Traditions), 2007, p. 157: "The figure of Yeshua thus remains a multifaceted diamond whose totality none can grasp. In spite of their divergences, the gospels are not opposed but are instead complementary. The views of Judas, Miriam, Yohanan, and Matthew form an ensemble that witnesses to the same presence of Yeshua – infinitely close, yet ungraspable. How many more gospels would be needed to reveal the full brilliance of this diamond?"

Chapter Five

[1]Cf. Acts 9:2; 19:9, 23; 24:14, 22.

²Cf. Mattison, *Judas,* p. 47.

³Cynthia Bourgeault, *The Wisdom Way of Knowing: Reclaiming an Ancient Tradition to Awaken the Heart* (Jossey-Bass), 2003, pp. xvii, xviii.

⁴Cf. Mattison, *Mary,* pp. 49-52.

⁵Bourgeault, *The Wisdom Jesus,* pp. 62ff.

⁶Cf. Mattison, *Thomas,* p. 24. In my colloquial translation of Thomas, I used the term "Ultimate Reality" instead of the more literal "kingdom of God." In this translation, however, I propose the more familiar term "God's Reign" as more reflective of Q's ambiguity.

⁷Quoted by Jeffrey F. Hambuger in Amy Hollywood and Patricia Z. Beckman, eds., *The Cambridge Companion to Christian Mysticism* (Cambridge University Press), 2012, p. 286.

⁸Daniel C. Matt, *"Ayin:* The Concept of Nothingness in Jewish Mysticism," *Tikkun,* Vol. 3, No. 3., p. 45.

⁹Cf. Mattison, *Mary,* p. 45; *Thomas,* pp. 12-13; 24.

¹⁰David A. Cooper, *God is a Verb: Kabbalah and the Practice of Mystical Judaism* (Riverhead Books), 1997, p. 134.

Bibliography

Arnal, William, "The Q Document," in Matt Jackson-McCabe, ed., *Jewish Christianity Reconsidered: Rethinking Ancient Groups and Texts* (Fortress), 2007, pp. 119-154

Borg, Marcus J., *Jesus: Uncovering the Life, Teachings, and Relevance of a Religious Revolutionary* (HarperSanFrancisco), 2006

Borg, Marcus, *The Lost Gospel Q: The Original Sayings of Jesus* (Ulysses Press), 1996

Bourgeault, Cynthia, *The Wisdom Jesus: Transforming Heart and Mind – a New Perspective on Christ and His Message* (Shambhala), 2008

Bourgeault, Cynthia, *The Wisdom Way of Knowing: Reclaiming an Ancient Tradition to Awaken the Heart* (Jossey-Bass), 2003

Cooper, David A., *God is a Verb: Kabbalah and the Practice of Mystical Judaism* (Riverhead Books), 1997

DeConick, April D., *The Thirteenth Apostle: What the Gospel of Judas Really Says* (Continuum), 2007, rev. ed. 2009

Dewey, Arthur J. and Miller, Robert J., *The Complete Gospel Parallels* (Polebridge Press), 2012

Ehrman, Bart D., *The Historical Jesus: Part I* (The Teaching Company), 2000

Hambuger, Jeffrey F., "Mysticism and Visuality," in Amy Hollywood and Patricia Z. Beckman, eds., *The Cambridge Companion to Christian Mysticism* (Cambridge University Press), 2012

Herzog, William R. II, *Jesus, Justice, and the Reign of God: A Ministry of Liberation* (Westminster John Knox Press), 2000

Kloppenborg, John S., "On Dispensing with Q? Goodacre on the Relation of Luke to Matthew," *New Testament Studies*, 2003, Vol. 49, pp. 210-236

Kloppenborg, John S., *The Formation of Q: Trajectories in Ancient Wisdom Collections* (Fortress), 1987

Leloup, Jean-Yves, *Judas and Jesus: Two Faces of a Single Revelation* (Inner Traditions), 2007

Matt, Daniel C., *"Ayin:* The Concept of Nothingness in Jewish Mysticism," *Tikkun*, Vol. 3, No. 3., pp. 43-47

Mattison, Mark M., *The Gospel of Judas: The Sarcastic Gospel* (CreateSpace Independent Publishing Platform), 2014

Mattison, Mark M., *The Gospel of Mary: A Fresh Translation and Holistic Approach* (CreateSpace Independent Publishing Platform), 2013

Mattison, Mark M., *The Gospel of Thomas: A New Translation for Spiritual Seekers* (CreateSpace Independent Publishing Platform), 2015

Miller, Robert J., ed., *The Complete Gospels: Fourth Edition* (Polebridge Press), 2010

Orlando, Robert, *Apostle Paul: A Polite Bribe* (Cascade Books), 2014

Robinson, James M., Hoffman, Paul, and Kloppenborg, John S., eds., *The Critical Edition of Q: Synopsis including the Gospels of Matthew and Luke, Mark and Thomas with English, German, and French Translations of Q and Thomas* (Peeters), 2000

Wright, N.T., *The New Testament and the People of God* (Fortress), 1992

Wright, N.T., *Jesus and the Victory of God* (Fortress), 1996

Made in United States
Orlando, FL
20 November 2024

54215163R00039